Did I Tell You
I Love You Today?

a true story about how a heart grew...

inspired by
Poodie

illustrated and written by
Rose Petruzzi

First edition

Library of Congress Control Number: 2009908575

Publisher's Cataloging-In-Publication Data

Petruzzi, Rosemary.
Did I tell you I love you today? : a true story about how a heart grew / illustrated and written by Rose Petruzzi. -- 1st ed.

p. : col. ill. ; cm.

"Inspired by Poodie."
Summary: A true story of how a heart grew. Poodie, a rescued poodle, inspires us to acknowledge our gifts and the beauty around us, and connect to the joy in our hearts. She helps us to remember and be thankful for the simple, yet not so simple, miracles in our everyday lives.
Interest age level: 002-006.
ISBN-13: 978-0-9842027-0-6
ISBN-10: 0-9842027-0-6

1. Dog owners--Psychology--Juvenile literature. 2. Gratitude--Juvenile literature.
3. Love--Juvenile literature. 4. Dogs. 5. Gratitude. 6. Love. I. Title.

PZ10.3.P48 Di 2009   2009908575
[E]

Published by Poodie Productions, Bethlehem, Connecticut
Printed in the United States of America in North Mankato, Minnesota
www.repetruzzi.com
Production Date: 082709
Batch Number: 1-1-1000-82709-pp

This book is dedicated to You,
with great love, joy and gratitude...

There once was a
spectacular being...

...A warm, fuzzy being at that, named Pood.

Pood knew her purpose since the day she was born, and that was to love.

She lives what is in her heart,
and simply thinks,
or sometimes says...

"Did I tell You I love you today?"

3

4

Did I tell You I love you this morning
when I opened my eyes to see you?

6

Did I tell You I love you
for creating me just the way I am?

8

Did I tell You I love you
for so generously providing me
everything I need?

10

Did I tell You
I love you today
because my heart
sings with joy?

12

Did I tell You today
that I love you
for helping me grow?

Did I tell You I love You today
for feeling One
with all Your creations?

Did I tell You I love you today for all the beauty that surrounds us?

18

19

Did I tell You
I love you today
for making this earth,
our home,
a paradise?

20

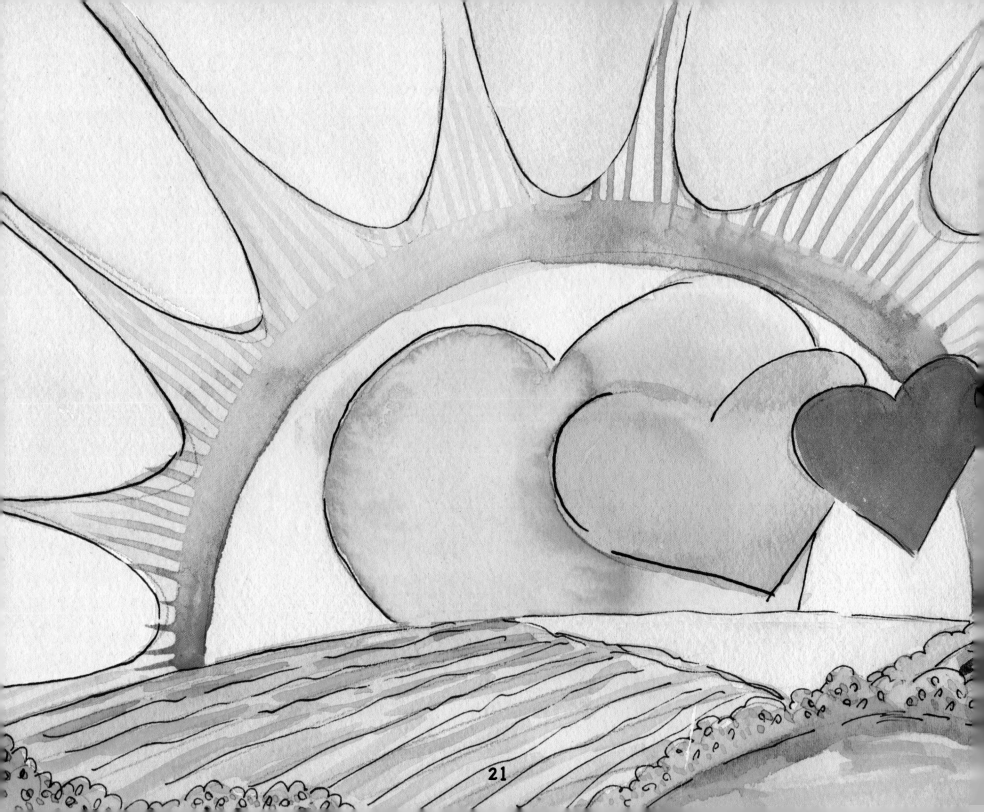

Did I thank You today
for all Your great gifts?

22

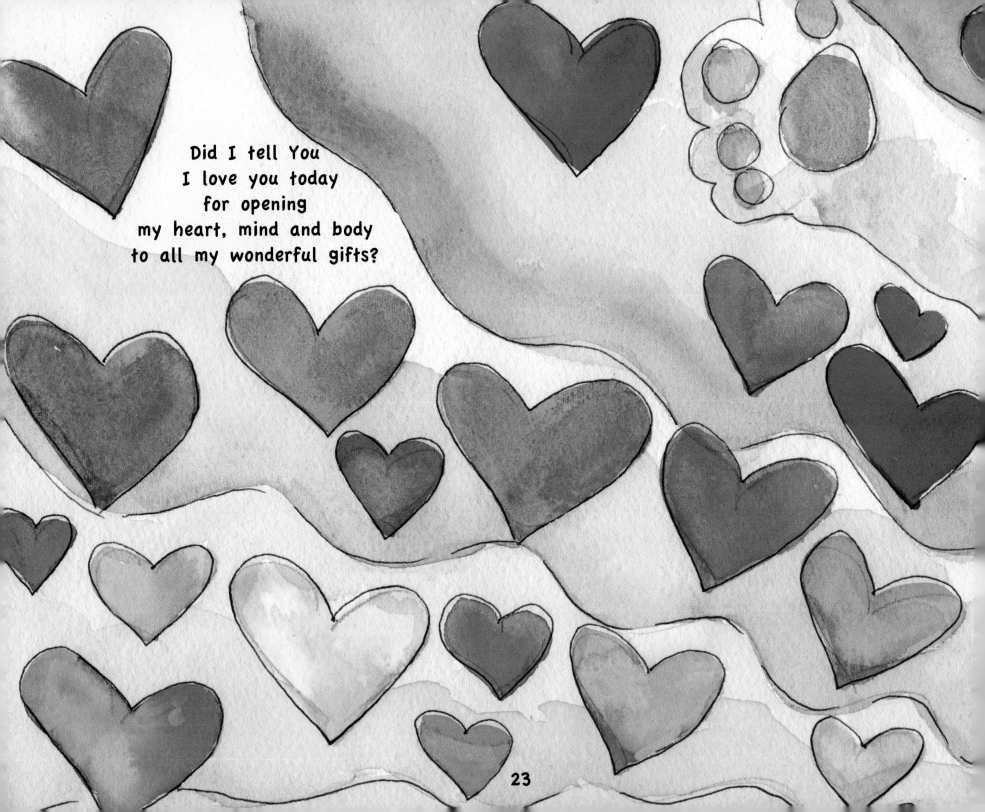

Did I tell You
I love you today
for opening
my heart, mind and body
to all my wonderful gifts?

23

Did I tell You I love you today
because you are here with me?

26

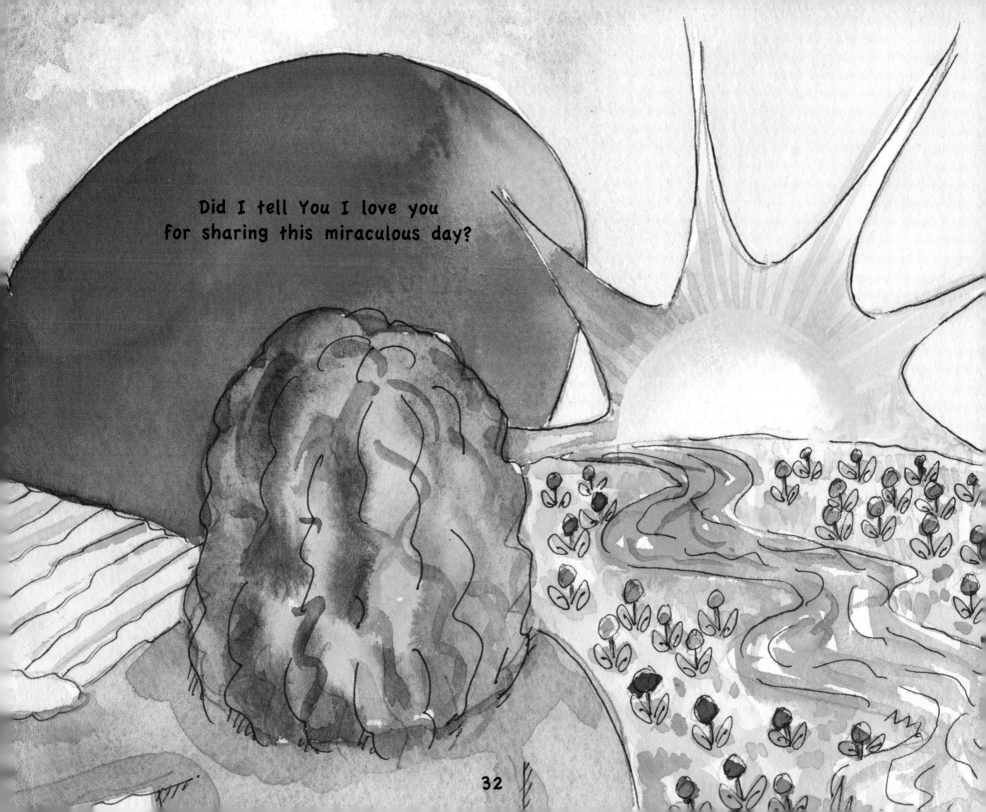

Did I thank You today...

33

...for all Your love?

34

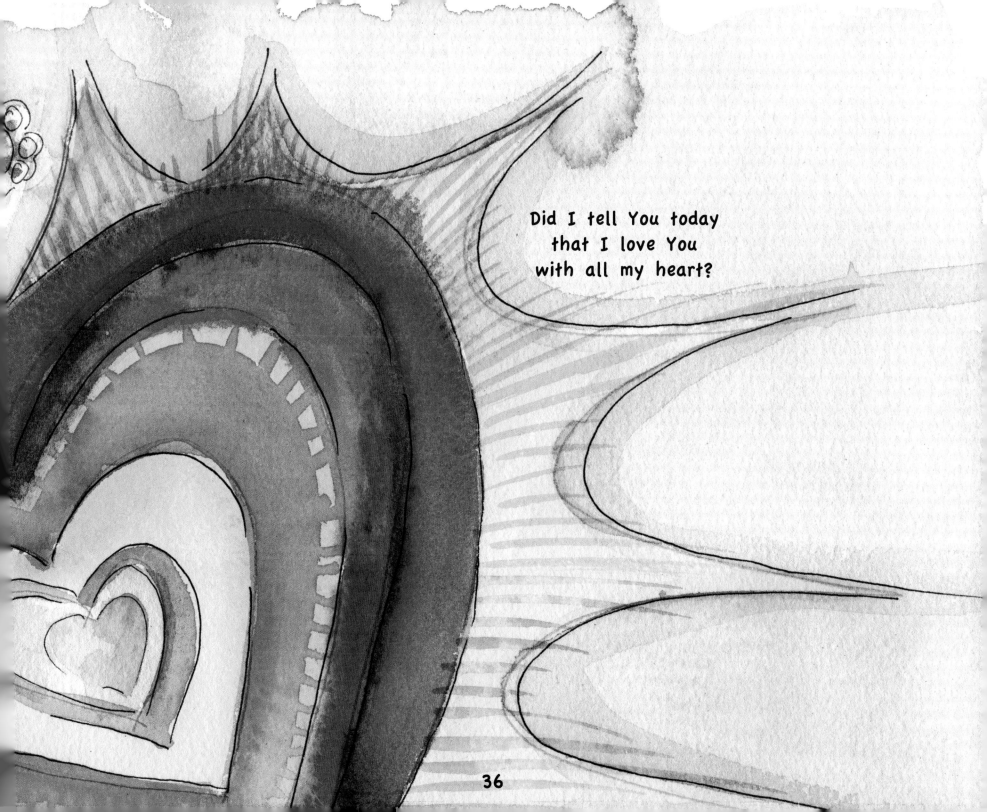

About Pood

"Poodie" was the brainchild of Rose's husband, Chris Cocozza, in the spring of 2001. Having grown up with poodles, he knew how wonderful it was to have a canine member of the family. So he went looking for a dog to rescue. He found Poodie, a cowering, aloof two-year-old miniature poodle with soulful eyes.

Pood learned to adapt to her new home and eventually became a major influence in the lives of both Rose and Chris. Her gentle, steady, unconditional love is a constant reminder of forces at work greater than ourselves. She nudges us to look at ourselves, our world, and our lives with gratitude, to appreciate all that has been given to us.

Special thanks to Chris Cocozza, Jan Prenoveau, Nicole Lilley, and my editor Virginia Small, for all your support.

Most of all, I'd like to thank Poodie, the co-creator of this dream come true. I love you!

Rose

Poodie's Valentine's Day portrait

Poodie sniffing her favorite flower

Poodie saying hello